W9-CDZ-573

Pebble®

My World

Neighborhoods
in My World

by Ella Cane

Consulting Editor: Gail Saunders-Smith, PhD

CAPSTONE PRESS
a capstone imprint

Pebble Books are published by Capstone Press,
1710 Roe Crest Drive, North Mankato, Minnesota 56003
www.capstonepub.com

Copyright © 2014 by Capstone Press, a Capstone imprint. All rights reserved.
No part of this publication may be reproduced in whole or in part, or stored in a
retrieval system, or transmitted in any form or by any means, electronic, mechanical,
photocopying, recording, or otherwise, without written permission of the publisher.

Library of Congress Cataloging-in-Publication Data
Cane, Ella.
Neighborhoods in my world / by Ella Cane.
pages cm. — (Pebble books. My world)
Includes index.
Audience: K to Grade 3.
ISBN 978-1-4765-3119-9 (library binding)
ISBN 978-1-4765-3461-9 (paperback)
ISBN 978-1-4765-3467-1 (ebook pdf)
1. Neighborhoods—Juvenile literature. I. Title.
HT152.C36 2014
307.3′362—dc23   2013005893

Summary: Simple text and full-color photographs introduce the people and places
of a neighborhood to the reader.

Note to Parents and Teachers

The My World set supports national curriculum standards
for social studies related to people, places, and environments.
This book describes and illustrates neighborhoods. The images
support early readers in understanding the text. The repetition
of words and phrases helps early readers learn new words.
This book also introduces early readers to subject-specific
vocabulary words, which are defined in the Glossary section.
Early readers may need assistance to read some words and to
use the Table of Contents, Glossary, Read More, Internet Sites,
and Index sections of the book.

Printed in the United States of America in North Mankato, Minnesota.
032013   007223CGF13

Table of Contents

What Is a Neighborhood?

People work and live
in neighborhoods.
A neighborhood is the area
around a person or place.

My Neighborhood

I live in a suburb.

My neighborhood has many homes.

Places in My Neighborhood

At the park I play with

Jess and Mason.

They are my neighbors.

Our school is
in our neighborhood.
I walk to school
with Lila and Ben.

We visit the post office
in our neighborhood.
We mail packages
and letters.

Other Neighborhoods

One town can have
many neighborhoods.
They can be big or small,
new or old.

Big cities have
crowded neighborhoods.
Buildings sit close together.

Rural neighborhoods
are not crowded.
Homes may be far away
from other homes.

Who are the people,
and what are the places
in your neighborhood?

Glossary

neighbor—a person who lives near or next door to the person speaking

post office—a building where people go to buy stamps and send letters and packages

rural—having to do with the countryside or farming

suburb—a town or village very close to a city

town—a group of neighborhoods that form a community; towns are small parts of a state

Read More

Lyons, Shelly. *People in My Neighborhood.* My Neighborhood. North Mankato, Minn.: Capstone Press, 2013.

Morris, Neil. *Communities.* Investigate. Chicago: Heinemann Library, 2010.

Owens, L. L. *Meet Your Neighborhood.* Let's Be Social. Edina, Minn.: Magic Wagon, 2011.

Internet Sites

FactHound offers a safe, fun way to find Internet sites related to this book. All of the sites on FactHound have been researched by our staff.

Here's all you do:

Visit *www.facthound.com*

Type in this code: 9781476531199

Check out projects, games and lots more at
www.capstonekids.com

Index

Word Count: 115
Grade: 1
Early-Intervention Level: 14

Editorial Credits
Shelly Lyons, editor; Juliette Peters, designer; Marcie Spence, media researcher; Eric Manske, production specialist

Photo Credits
Alamy Images: Bradley Sauter, 12; Capstone Studio: Karon Dubke, 8, 10, 20; Shutterstock: Anne Kitzman, 18, deckard_73, 1, Felix Mizioznikov, 4, Pablo Scapinachis, cover (front), Tim Roberts Photography, 14, trekandshoot, 6, Triff, cover (background), Vacclav, 16